DRESSED

Forget the big girl panties. It's time to suit up in the powerful armor that's custom-tailored for every woman who follows Jesus.

POLLY BALINT

Trilogy Christian Publishers
A Wholly Owned Subsidiary of Trinity Broadcasting Network
2442 Michelle Drive
Tustin, CA 92780

For information about special discounts for bulk purchases, please contact Trilogy Christian Publishing.
Manufactured in the United States of America

10 9 8 7 6 5 4 3 2 1
Library of Congress Cataloging-in-Publication Data is available.
ISBN 979-8-89041-196-9
ISBN (ebook) 979-8-89041-197-6

REVIEWS

Wow!! Polly delivers such grace and insight in this study! As a woman who is an avid reader, I found this to be structured so well, very easy to follow and understand. You are engaged from the beginning and feel a sense of joy and peace as you complete the sessions. Ladies will find themselves encouraging one another in new and practical ways as they walk through the pages of this workbook. Polly Balint truly has a gift when she guides and lifts women with true and relevant biblical teachings. Great study for women at all stages of life!!

—Cassandra Schneeberger

What an amazing and life changing Bible study this has been! I have read this same scripture many, many times in my life, but the way Polly puts it together makes the words jump right off the page for a wonderful life application. She makes this scripture come to life and is so detailed in what we need to do daily to put on the armor of God. Going through this study is definitely a life changing experience!

—Natalie Rose Brown

"A totally dressed woman takes God at His word and finds strength." Polly's insightful biblical unpacking of how to achieve victory in spiritual warfare is a "must read" for every Christian woman doing battle today. Read it, share it. "Put it on!"

—Deborah Rey

Polly has written a powerful and impactful Bible study that illuminates the armor of God in a new and profound way. She has used passages from all throughout the Bible to lead the reader to a deeper understanding of each piece of the armor, and why it's so desperately needed in the daily struggle to defeat the enemy. I have been encouraged, convicted, and challenged that I haven't been walking in all the victory God has for me because I'm not getting totally dressed in the armor that He's generously gifted me. Now I'm ready to step out each day fully equipped for battle as a mighty warrior for God!

—Michelle Wenzel

What do I wear today? Polly helps us to dress in a "war-drobe" to empower us every day. She opens Ephesians 6:10-18 in its message that will dress us all in a style to conquer the evil we face today. Having that extra strength will carry you to the next level of your faith. Polly's love of the Lord and spirit-filled energy are felt throughout her book to keep you Totally Dressed as you learn to put on God's "war-drobe" daily.

--Pat Stephens

"Practically Perfect" from Polly! Once again Polly has given a gift to her sisters in Christ through her new Bible study *Totally Dressed.* Passing on her own confidence in Christ and her love for God's Word, Polly expounds on how sisters can be *Totally Dressed* in the haute couture God has specially designed for His children in spiritual warfare. Praise be to God for such perfect armor and for Polly's passion for helping "Sisters" get *Totally Dressed.*

—Marion K. Tims, EdS

Just as Polly has cheered many of us along in our walk with Christ, she's encouraging us again in *Totally Dressed* to go deeper in our walk with Christ and be fully equipped when the enemy comes against us.

—Julie Joiner Tubbs

The Lord has given my dear friend Polly the special gift of writing about and teaching His Word. In her latest project from the book of Ephesians, Polly explains each piece of His designer wardrobe perfectly and why it is essential that we wear it every day. Today, we are in a spiritual battle like never before, and *Totally Dressed* is the battle plan we need.

—Tracy Marshall

DEDICATION

To God,

What a loving Father You are! You created women and fully equipped us to be fierce and fragile world-changing nurturers for Your glory! You tell us, “Do not be overcome by evil, but overcome evil with good.” (Romans 12:21)

To the Totally Dressed woman,

“Women who follow Jesus don’t just rock cradles. We are meant to rock the world with all the love and hope and Holy Spirit power inside each one of us. We are global, from every tribe, tongue, generation, and nation. We were born to nurture, born to be wild with the power of His love, all for the glory of God.” (*NURTURE,* Polly Balint, pg. 75). “Remember, the devil does not have a shield, but we do!” (*NURTURE*, pg. 90). His name is Jesus.

To my loving family and friends,

I thank you with all my heart for the countless ways you continue to encourage me through your love and prayers.

To the wonderful Trilogy Christian Publishing team,

Once again, you have blessed me and helped me with your professionalism, kindness, and encouragement, and I thank God for each of you.

INTRODUCTION

This isn't just playing "dress up."

The battle is real! Think supernaturally!

This 10-week study was written for the glory of God and with the desire to encourage women that (1) we (yes, we!) are not alone in the struggles we face every day, and (2) God has already given us everything we need to overcome the darkness of our daily battles.

Come on, let's start something! He's given us a supernatural outerwear called the armor of God, and it's not found in any mall, either. Nope. To make **this** kind of fashion statement we will only find this awesome attire in the pages of the Holy Scriptures. As we study **Ephesians 6:10-18** we'll learn that we will be putting on a covering that God has hand-tailored for each one of us. It comes with instructions that tell us what piece goes on first and where to fasten it. We'll also see how the Lord, in His unconditional love and wisdom, tells us to put on the **whole** armor of God so we can be "strong in the Lord and in His mighty power." (Ephesians 6:10). He has not left anything out and He does not want us to, either.

There is a spiritual war going on between the light and the darkness. Let me guess...you're tired and you have battle fatigue. Let's decide to get right with God, to begin believing Him and His Word and then act on it! The truth is: there is help and there is hope and it comes from a deep and abiding relationship with God.

It's my prayer that as we examine the supernatural wardrobe we will see in a new way the thoughtfulness and lovingkindness of God, our Commanding Officer. May we march together with hearts connected to Christ. May we encourage each other to dive deep into His word as one spiritual army and then stand our ground. Then we will see that the Lord God Himself is more awesome than we could ever dream!

Love, Polly

TABLE OF CONTENTS

SESSION ONE

"Finally, be strong in the Lord and in His mighty power."
Ephesians 6:10

When God created us He had a specific plan and purpose for each one of us. He knew ahead of time that we would have lots of needs and He provided for every single one—ahead of time! One of our needs is to have **protection from our** enemy—Satan or the devil–who is also God's enemy! Let that sink in...he is God's enemy, too! That should encourage us immediately. We're not in this alone. The devil is God's enemy, too. And God is with **us**!

Joshua 1:5 – *"No one will be able to stand up against you all the days of your life. As I was with Moses, so I will be with you; I will never leave you or forsake you."*

And God has provided for His children in several powerful ways. He's given us:

- **Himself:** His presence in our lives (Psalm 139:7-8)
- **Our Savior Jesus Christ**: our Rock, Refuge, Strength, the Lover of our Souls (Psalm 18:2-3)
- **The Holy Spirit**: to guide us and comfort us (John 14:25-26)
- **His Word:** to teach us (Hebrews 4:12)
- **Prayer**: to sustain us (Matthew 7:7-8)
- **Spiritual Armor**: to resist a spiritual enemy. (Ephesians 6:11)

But the thing is: for any of this to be effective, WE HAVE TO PUT IT ON! For the spiritual armor to protect us we have to get dressed!

But first we have to undress!

We have to take off **self** and put on **Christ**! That's where being strong in the Lord comes in: we have to get **self** out of the way. Being strong in the Lord is loving Him deeply and serving Him faithfully and passionately. And we can't do that until we believe God loves us. Even He wants us to get our self out of the way so His love can flow through us and He can live through us.

Take God at His Word. If God says it, then that settles it! Keep marching!

Matthew 16:24—

John 15:5b—

John 15:12—

"According to God's Word, the truth is that we were created in the image of God, that He loves us and that we are precious to Him. However, we do not bestow that worth onto ourselves...When Jesus tells us to love our neighbors as ourselves, the point is not that we need to learn to love ourselves so that we can love others. Jesus is saying we need to give others the same attention and care we give ourselves. We need to learn how to deny ourselves, so we can do that which does not come naturally – to truly love God and others. Once we have received His love, we will not have to compare ourselves to others; we will not focus on self at all. Instead , we will become channels of His love to others."1

To be strong in God is to BELIEVE God. Believe what His Word says. Believe He is who He says He is. Believe His promises. Believe!

1 John 5:4-5—

John speaks of two aspects of victory: 1--The initial victory of turning in faith from the world to God ("has overcome") and 2—the continuing day-by-day victory of Christian living ("overcomes the world"). To overcome the world is to gain victory over its sinful pattern of life, which is another way of describing obedience to God. Such obedience is not impossible for believers because they have been born again and the Holy Spirit dwells in them and gives them strength. [2]

John 10:10—

John 1:9—

God knows. He knows what we are going through. He knows what makes us struggle. He knows how we feel. He knows. Look at John 10:10 again. He has told us there is an enemy but to take heart, that He came to give us, His children, a richness and a fullnes of life that only He can give, in this life and the life to come.

A *totally dressed* woman takes God at His Word and finds strength.

1 John 4:4—

John 3:16—

Romans 5:8—

Now that's a LOT of love! Deep love!

We cannot be strong in ourselves. (Remember John 15:5?) We have a fierce and cruel enemy. The Apostle Paul wrote in the book of Ephesians: "Be strong in the Lord Jesus Christ."

Psalm 27:14—

Psalm 35:1, 4—

Psalm 37:34—

Psalm 105:4—

Believe God and take Him at His Word. Believe Him to be the provider of strength and power.

Matthew 28:18-20—

A *totally dressed* woman is a Proverbs 31 woman: "She is clothed in strength and dignity and can laugh at the days to come.[3]" (Proverbs 31:25) She can do that, not because **she's** so great, but because **her God is so great.** She believes God. She believes He is in control and she believes He will take care of her and all that concerns her. And as she puts on her spiritual armor she marches on in love, faithfulness, and joy.

Nancy Leigh DeMoss, *Lies Women Believe and the Truth That Sets Them Free, ©2001 Nancy Leigh DeMoss, (Moody Publishers, Chicago) pgs. 71-72.*

[2] *Zondervan NIV Study Bible*, ©2002 The Zondervan Corporation, Grand Rapids, MI, 49530

3 Zondervan NIV Study Bible, ©2002 The Zondervan Corporation, Grand Rapids, MI, 49530

Notes

SESSION TWO

"Put on the whole armor of God that you may be able to stand against the wiles of the devil. For our struggle is not against flesh and blood, but against the rulers, against the authorities, against the powers of this dark world and against the spiritual forces of evil in the heavenly realms."

Ephesians 6:11-12

"Put on the whole armor of God..."

"Not armor that God himself is sometimes clothed with and uses against his enemies, but what he has provided for is people. It is called *the armor of God*, because it is prepared by him for his people, and is bestowed on them by him; and because it is in its own nature divine and spiritual, and not carnal; and because it is provided for fighting the Lord's battles, and is used in them, and the efficacy [power and effectiveness] of it is from him and the execution it does is owing to him."[1] All glory and power go to Him alone for each victory!

We give God glory for His provision, His protection, and His power. Look what He is doing for us so that we are well-cared for – preparing us for the times of war and hardship. He's got us covered!

Zechariah 4:6-7 – "So the (angel of the Lord) said to me, 'This is the word of the LORD to Zerubbabel: **'Not by might nor by power, but by my Spirit,' says the Lord Almighty.'** What are you , O mighty mountain? Before Zerubbabel you will become level ground. Then He will bring out the capstone to shouts of 'God bless it! God bless it!'"[2]

Our God is a mountain mover. We need to spiritually get completely dressed in His all-powerful armor as He makes our mountains slide into the sea.

> *"The whole armor of God is whole, complete, and perfect; and all of it is useful, no part is to be neglected, but all is to be taken and 'put on'; which is not to make and provide this armor but to all to be taken and 'put on' to take it as being ready made and provided and to expect and prepare for battle, and make use of it.*

"And this supposes saints (God's people) to be in a warfare state, and that they are in the character of soldiers, and have enemies to fight with, and therefore should be clothed with proper and suitable armor to meet them!"[3] *(Emphasis added: mine!)*

Charles Spurgeon's description of Ephesians 6:11: "The apostle [Paul] represents the believer as a soldier, and urges him to prepare for the battle by taking to himself all defensive and offensive arms. Satan will assail every part of us, and therefore we need to be protected from head to foot like the knights of old."[4]

God knows our needs and He provides for every one!

2 Peter 1:3-4 – "His divine power has given us everything we need for life and godliness through our knowledge of Him who called us by His own glory and goodness. Through these things He has given us His very great and precious promises, so that through them you may participate in the divine nature and escape the corruption in the world caused by evil desires."

He will help us though our struggles. Our duty is to surrender ourselves to Him and willfully obey the voice of our Commanding Officer, the Lord Jesus Christ.

James 4:6—

James 4:7—

Oswald Chambers, in his devotional, *My Utmost for His Highest,* wrote: "We don't have to fight or wrestle *with* God, but we must wrestle before God *with things*. Beware of lazily giving up. Instead, put up a glorious fight and you will find yourself empowered with His strength."[5]

"...that you may be able to stand against the wiles of the devil."

We have to remember that our battle is a spiritual battle against an unseen enemy. John Gill calls him the "grand enemy of Christ and His people, and a very powerful and cunning one."

We are told to put on the whole armor of God—against all the enemy's might and craftiness—

in order to stand against him, oppose him, and fight, and get the victory over him, which is always obtained by believers; for they not only stand their ground in the strength of Christ, but confound his schemes and confuse his strategies, and are more than conquerers through Him who has loved them.

"If we fought with men we might be less guarded; wrestling as we do with subtle and spiritual adversaries, whose weapons are as mysterious as they are deadly, it becomes us to be **doubly watchful** lest in some unguarded point we receive wounds which will bleed for years."[6]

Ephesians 5:15-16—

1 Peter 5:8—

"Self-control" is a fruit of the Spirit.

1 Peter 1:13—

1 Thessalonians 5:6, 8—

God is omnipresent. He is omniscient. He is watching over us. 2 Chronicles 16:9 states: "The eyes of the Lord range throughout the earth to strengthen those whose hearts are fully committed to Him." This is comforting and empowering. We should be encouraged to persevere knowing He is always watching over us. We will take our stand and keep standing (persevere) as we put all our trust and hope in Him.

When David faced Goliath, he was fully clothed in the *spiritual* armor of God. In comparison, at nine feet tall, Goliath was wearing a bronze helmet, bronze coat, bronze javelin, bronze covering his legs, and his shield bearer went out before him. (1 Samuel 17:5-7)

David told King Saul he would fight the giant. (1 Samuel 17:32) "The LORD who delivered me from the paw of the lion and the paw of the bear will deliver me from the hand of this

Philistine." (1 Samuel 17:37)

Saul gave David his armor to wear and David chose not to wear it. (1 Samuel 17:39-40) He was already wearing the **full armor of God** and he defeated his enemy "in the name of the Lord Almighty." (1 Samuel 17:45)

The account of King Jehoshapat in **2 Chronicles 20** is another powerful testimony in Scripture of submitting to God, dressing in the full armor of God, and then taking a firm stand. Moabites, Ammonites, and Meunites came to make war on Jehoshaphat. He was told that a vast army was coming.

V. 3 –4 – Alarmed, Jehoshaphat resolved to inquire of the LORD, and proclaimed a fast for Judah. The people of Judah came together to seek help from the LORD;

V. 5 – Then Jehoshaphat stood up in the assembly and prayed with great faith:

V. 14 – 15 – Then the Spirit of the Lord came upon Jahaziel son of Zechariah.... "This is what the Lord says to you, "Do not be afraid or discouraged because of this vast army. For the battle is not yours but God's. ...

V. 17 – You will not have to fight this battle. Take up your positions; stand firm and see the deliverance the LORD will give you, ...do not be afraid ; do not be discouraged. Go out and face them tomorrow, and the LORD will be with you.

Jehoshaphat bowed before the LORD and they began to praise and worship the LORD. Early the next day, he told them to have faith and believe God and God's promises to them. They went out to war with praise!

V. 22 – As they began to sing and praise, the LORD set ambushes against the men of Ammon and Moab and Mount Seir who were invading Judah and they were defeated. The enemies began to destroy each other.

V. 24 – When the men of Judah came to the place that overlooks the desert and looked toward the vast army they only saw dead bodies on the ground.

V. 25 – So Jehoshaphat and his men went to carry off their plunder, and they found among them a great amount of equipment and clothing and also articles of value....more than they could take away. There was so much plunder that it took three days to collect it.

God is faithful! Look at what He has done. Amazing. Now is the time for God's daughters to "RISE & SHINE" and to "commit our way to the LORD; trust in Him and He will do this: He will make our righteousness shine like the dawn, the justice of our cause like the noonday sun." 7

John Gill, *Gill's Commentary*, Vol. 6, Ephesians 6:11, page 456, Baker Book House, Grand Rapids, MI, 1980.

[2] *Zondervan NIV Study Bible*, © 2002 The Zondervan Corporation, Grand Rapids, MI, 49530

[3]John Gill, *Gill's Commentary*, Vol. 6, Ephesians 6:11, page 456, Baker Book House, Grand Rapids, MI, 1980.

[4] Charles H. Spurgeon, *Spurgeon's Devotional Bible*, Baker Books, Grand Rapids, MI 1998.

[5] Oswald Chambers, *My Utmost for His Highest Updated Graduate Edition, Eph. 6/Dec. 16,* Discovery House © 1995 OC Publications Ltd.

[6] Charles H. Spurgeon, *Spurgeon's Devotional Bible*, pg. 712 Baker Books, Grand Rapids, MI 1998.

[7] Psalm 37:5-6, *Zondervan NIV Study Bible*, © 2002 The Zondervan Corporation, Grand Rapids, MI, 49530

"For our struggle is not against flesh and blood..."

"[The Apostle] Paul's scope in Ephesians has been cosmic. From the very beginning he has drawn attention to the unseen world and now he describes the spiritual battle that takes place against evil in the 'heavenly realms.'" [1]

We are told to be strong in the Lord ***(Ephesians 6:10),*** to put on the full armor of God ***(Ephesians 6:11),*** and prepare for battle, because our enemies are not "flesh and blood." The Apostle Paul tells us that our struggles, or "wrestling", is not the kind of wrestling alluded to in the Olympic Games, but this wrestling is similar to Jacob's wrestling; it's not of the body but of the soul.[2]

This is spiritual wrestling.

Matthew 16:17—

Galatians 1:15-16—

Although in this world we do have battles with those who are irreverent, profane, and disrespectful, but we wrestle against them with our spiritual armor: by bearing a testimony against their darkness, by enduring their attacks, and overcome them by clinging to Christ in faith which gives us victory over them. We also overcome them by using Scripture to disprove them. This is our spiritual armor.

We are not to fight as the world fights: with violence, anger, intimidation, and terrorism. We are cautioned by the Apostle Paul <u>not</u> to:

- lash out against human opponents as though they were the real enemy;
- assume that the battle can be fought using merely human resources.

"But against the powers of this dark world;"

Our struggles are over wicked men in this dark world, who are in a state of darkness itself; and so Satan is called the prince, and god of the world. 3

John 12:31—

The cross was God's judgement on the world. The prince of this world is Satan. The cross would seem to be his triumph but it was in fact, his defeat. Out of it would flow the greatest good ever to come to the world. 4

2 Corinthians 4:4—

The god of this age is the devil, who is the archenemy of God and the unseen power behind all unbelief and ungodliness. Those who follow him have in effect made him their god. "This present age" is characterized by wickedness.

It was common use among the Jews to call the devil "prince of darkness", "angel of death" , and "the darkness of this world"; and they also used that phrase of civil governors – so the phrase was also "rulers of the world."[5]

"Against spiritual forces of evil in the heavenly realms."

These wicked spirits are unclean, proud, lying, deceitful, and malicious. They are said to be in "high" or "heavenly places"; but that does not mean super celestial, or in the highest heavens-- the third heaven where God, the angels and the saints are – but in the aerial heavens, where the power or posse of devils reside. They are above us, over our heads, overlooking us, and watching for every advantage against us; and therefore we should have on our armor, and be in a readiness to engage them "in the air" [spiritually speaking]. 6

This graphic description by John Gill is just another confirmation of what God has already told us—to get up and get dressed in the full armor. We must be wearing our armor. Gill's description is insightful, too, and reminds us that we have a loving God who, by His grace, gives us protection through His gift of the spiritual armor.

Ephesians 1:3—

Ephesians 1: 10—

2 Corinthians 4:6-7—

Deuteronomy 20:3-4—

Women can be concerned about wearing the right outfit for the right season. Well, guess what? Dressing in the full armor of God IS the right ensemble and it will NEVER go out of style from season to season to season. We need to daily put it on in faith and bring Him glory!

John Gill, *Gill's Commentary*, Vol. 6, Eph. 6:12, pg. 456, 1980 Baker Book House, Grand Rapids. MI.

[2] John Gill, *Gill's Commentary*, Vol. 6, Eph. 6:12, pg. 456, 1980 Baker Book House, Grand Rapids. MI.

[3] John Gill, *Gill's Commentary*, Vol. 6, Eph. 6:12, pg. 456, 1980 Baker Book House, Grand Rapids. MI.

[4] *Zondervan NIV Study Bible, © 2002* The Zondervan Corp., Grand Rapids, MI. commentary on John 12:31

[5]John Gill, *Gill's Commentary*, Vol. 6, 66

[6] John Gill, *Gill's Commentary*, Vol. 6

Notes

SESSION THREE

"Therefore, put on the full armor of God, so that when the day of evil comes,you may be able to stand your ground, and after you have done everything,to stand."

Ephesians 6:13

This verse is repeated from Ephesians 6:11. Repetition seems necessary because of the many powerful enemies mentioned in the preceding verse, and serves to explain what is meant by putting it on.[1] This command leads the Apostle Paul to give an account of the several parts of this armor to enable the soldier to stand.

" ...so that when the day of evil comes, you may be able to stand your ground and having done all to stand..."

In this context the imagery is not that of a massive invasion of the domain of evil, but of individual soldiers withstanding assault.[2] By wearing the full armor of God, the warrior is able to stand against Satan's strategies, agendas, wickedness, his power and his might; oppose his schemes and resist his temptations.

We are then enabled to "face him, and give him battle, being suited with the whole armor of God....in the evil day when sin and iniquity abound, error and heresy prevail, Satan is very busy, trials and afflictions come on, persecution arises because of the Word, and God's judgements are in the earth."[3]

In the midst of such evil and warfare, we **can** stand on the Word of God and His promises to His people!

Isaiah 55:10-11—

Psalm 107:20—

Psalm 147:15—

Psalm 33:4—

Under the Lord's rule by His sovereign "Word", His plans for His people "Stand firm", even as the creation order "stood firm" because of being ordered by His sovereign "Word". Hence, His chosen people are a blessed nation.[4]

Psalm 18:32-35—

2 Timothy 1:7—

This is a call to be faithful and to believe God and take Him at His Word. We must focus on our Savior instead of our circumstances.

"Turn your eyes upon Jesus
Look full in His wonderful face
And the things of this earth will grow strangely dim
In the light of His glory and grace."[5]

So as we stand, we overcome, having routed the enemy, stand as conquerers; or rather, having taken and put on the whole armor of God, in order to stand, and withstand the enemy.[6]

When we persevere we prove the devil is a liar. God wants us to stand in faith and give Him glory by standing and believing Him.

John Gill, *Gill's Commentary, Vol. 6, Eph.6:13,* ©1980 Baker Book House, Grand Rapids, MI.

[2] *Zondervan NIV Study Bible,* commentary on Eph. 6:13

[3] John *Gill's Commentary, Vol. 6.*

[4] *Zondervan NIV Study Bible,* commentary on Psalm 33:4

[5] Turn Your Eyes Upon Jesus by Helen H. Lemmel 1922

[6] John Gill, *Gill's Commentary, Vol. 6.*

Notes

SESSION FOUR

"Stand firm, then, with the belt of truth buckled around your waist..."

Ephesians 6:14

This passage of Scripture repeats the exhortation to "stand", and as we seek to obey this command, the grace of God continues to watch over us and cover us. Only the Lord God Almighty is able to keep us standing. He keeps His Word!

His loving command is for us to "keep your ground, do not desert the army, the church of Christ, nor His cause; continue in the station in which you are placed, keep your post, be upon your watch, stand upon your guard."[1]

"...with the belt of truth buckled around your waist..."

The belt of truth is the gospel and all the doctrines of it:

John 14:6—

Ephesians 1:13—

Ephesians 4:15—

Charles Spurgeon, in his commentary, reminds us that the spiritual belt completely surrounds the body for our protection: "A girdle[belt] of sincerity[truth] keeps the whole man in marching order, and braces him up to meet the father of lies. An insincere man is a loose man, and a loose man is a lost man."[2]

In His love and wisdom God instructs us to have the spiritual belt of truth *buckled* around our waist, and we should realize He is telling us we must not be separated from it. This keeps us close to God and to Christ and it will "strengthen us against the assaults and attacks of Satan; and is of great use in the Christians' spiritual conflict with their enemies."[3]

Look at this: the first piece of armor we are told to put on is the belt of **truth**. It sounds like an anchor and a foundation, doesn't it? And it's not a coincidence that the enemy is called "the father of lies" (John 8:44).

2 Timothy 2:15—

Luke 8:11-15 (also Matthew 13 & Mark 4) is describing a farmer sowing seed. Jesus is explaining the meaning of the parable: God is the farmer and the seed is the Word of God. After He shares this truth in a parable, He instructs them in the following verse:

Luke 8:18—

The disciples heard not only for themselves but also for those to whom they would minister. Truth that is not understood and appropriated will be lost, but truth that is used will be multiplied.[4]

James 1:22—

We have great privileges as well as great responsibilities as God's children. **One of the privileges** is found in:

Luke 8:10-11—

This quote is from Isaiah.6:9 and does not express a desire that some would not understand, but simply states the sad truth that those who are not willing to receive Jesus' message will find the truth hidden from them.[5]

One of the responsibilities is:

That God has given us truth to live by and to share with others. What are we doing with this living truth? Forgetting about it? Studying it? Memorizing it? Sharing it with others? Mentoring? Are you willing to become a Titus 2 woman? (See Titus 2: 3-5.)

John 8:31-32—

The truth has the power to overcome every lie. That is what the enemy doesn't want you[us] to realize. As long as you[we] believe his lies, he can keep you[us] in bondage. But once you [we] know the Truth and start believing and acting on it, the prison doors will swing open and you [we] will be set free.[6]

John 8:36—

Romans 6:17-18—

Wholeheartedly obeyed—Christian obedience is not forced or legalistic, but willing.

Form of teaching – may refer to a summary of the moral and ethical teachings of Christ that was given to new converts in the early church.

Slaves to righteousness – Christians have changed masters. Whereas they were formerly slaves to sin, now they become slaves (willing servants) to righteousness.[7]

So how do we *"stand firm, then"* as it is written in Ephesians 6:14?

"On Christ the solid rock I stand All other ground is sinking sand."[8]

Matthew 7: 24-25 – Therefore everyone who hears these words of mine and puts them into practice is like a wise [wo]man who built [her] his house on a rock. The rain came down, the streams rose, and the winds blew and beat against that house; yet it did not fall, because it had its foundation on the rock.

It's time to take the pressure off ourselves to be our own savior. It's time to get dressed in the powerful suit God gave us and let's make a real "fashion" statement! Let's put on the belt of Truth and buckle it. It's time to rise <u>and</u> shine and bring glory to God!

3 John 4—

C.H. Spurgeon, *Spurgeon's Devotional Bible*, pg. 712, Baker Books, 1998.

[2] C.H Spurgeon, *Spurgeon's Devotional Bible*, 1998

[3] John Gill, *Gill's Commentary, Vol. 6, Eph. 6:14,* 1980 Baker Book House, Grand Rapids, MI

[4] *Zondervan NIV Study Bible*, Luke 8:18, ©2002 The Zondervan Corp. Grand Rapids, MI

[5] *Zondervan NIV Study Bible*, Luke 8:10

[6] Nancy Leigh DeMoss, *Lies Women Believe and the Truth That Sets Them Free*, pg.246.©2001, Moody, IL

[7] *Zondervan NIV Study Bible Commentary*, Romans 6:17-18

[8] My Hope Is Built on Nothing Less, by William Bradbury ©1834, Composer John Stainer 1837.

Notes

SESSION FIVE

"...with the breastplate of righteousness in place..."

Ephesians 6:14

This verse is an allusion to **Isaiah 59:17—18** -- *"He put on **righteousness as His breastplate**, and the helmet of salvation on His Head; He put on the garments of vengeance and wrapped himself in zeal as in a cloak. According to what they have done, so will He repay wrath to His enemies and retribution to His foes."* [1]

This is a reminder to us of God's love and grace toward His children, that He will defend us.

The Lord's armor is compared to the believer's armor in the battle against Satan in Ephesians 14. Character, not brute force, wins the battle just as in the case of Christ. So here, again, the warriors' character is their defense. God Himself is symbolically described as putting on a breastplate of righteousness when He goes forth to bring about justice.[2]

The righteousness described in Ephesians 6:14 is not works of righteousness done by men, but rather the graces of faith and love.[3]

1 Thessalonians 5:8—

In this passage the Apostle Paul does not consistently attach a particular virtue to each piece of armor; it is the general idea of equipment for battle that is pictured. Though faith has another "place" in the Christian armor, it seems best to understand this of the righteousness of Christ, which is attributed to God, and received by faith, is a guard against, and repels the accusations and charges of Satan, and is a security from all wrath and condemnation.[4]

Romans 13:12—

The breastplate of righteousness will guard the heart.[5]

Proverbs 4:23—

The righteousness of God – which comes from God — will protect the heart and blunt the edge of Satans's temptations which he aims at our souls. A breastplate never has a back plate. This means there is no provision for a retreat and we must never think of going back; we are bound to face the enemy.[6]

We overcome struggles by keeping our focus on our Lord, not on our personal circumstances. Author Elisabeth Elliot wrote, "Fear arises when we imagine that everything depends on us."[7]

Proverbs 21:21—

Proverbs 15:9—

Examples of righteousness: keeping the commands of the Lord, to be "after God's own heart."

Genesis 7:1—

Genesis 15:6—

Romans 1:17—

Romans 2:13—

1 Timothy 6:11-12—

1 Timothy 4:16—

How do we obey this command to put on the breastplate of righteousness?

Matthew 6:33—

In other words:

"...do not worry about your life.." (Matthew 6:25). Our Lord pointed out that from His standpoint it is absolutely unreasonable for us to be anxious, worrying about how we will live. Jesus did not say that the person who takes no thought for anything in his life is blessed – no, that person is a fool. But Jesus did teach that His disciple must make his relations with God the dominating focus of his life, and to be cautiously carefree about everything else in comparison to that.....Jesus is saying that the greatest concern of life is to place our relationship with God first, and everything else second.[8]

Throughout Scripture the Lord is inviting us into a supernatural relationship with Him. He says He will fight our battles. We only need to believe, obey, and get dressed!

---

[2] *Zondervan NIV Study Bible*, Ephesians 6: 14 & Isaiah 59:17.

[3] John Gill, *Gill's Commentary, Vol. 6,* © 1980 Baker Book House, Grand Rapids, MI

[4] John Gill, *Gill's Commentary, Vol. 6*

[5] Charles H. Spurgeon, *Spurgeon's Devotional Bible*, pg. 712, Baker Book House, Grand Rapids, MI

[6] Charles H. Spurgeon, *Spurgeon's Devotional Bible*, pg. 712.6

[7] Elisabeth Elliot, *author/missionary/speaker/ Good Reads Quotes*

[8]Oswald Chambers, *My Utmost for His Highest Updated Grad.*, 5/21, Discovery House Pub., Grand Rapids, MI

Notes

SESSION SIX

"...and with your feet fitted in the readiness that comes from the gospel of peace"

Ephesians 6:15

Please notice that every piece of spiritual armor has to do with Christ the Lord. We see His power help us to overcome our enemies, His blood save us, and His love carry us through. Jesus is called the "Prince of Peace" in Isaiah 9:6. We're going to see that "His rule will bring wholeness and well-being to individuals and to society."[1]

- Having "feet fitted" or "shod" in the gospel of peace is the provision of a solid base or foundation [gospel of Jesus Christ] for the Christian soldier to set his/her foot upon and stand fast on it.
- It's called the gospel of peace because it creates peaceable tempers and behavior and gives peace to distressed minds; it directs the way to eternal peace, and produces peace by the blood of Christ.[2]
- The gospel of peace produces a happy, calm, confidence; because the gospel has given us perfect peace, we shall march over the rough places of the way without becoming discontented or depressed.[3]

Let's look at:

Isaiah 26:3—

This is describing an abundance of peace that only comes from Christ. It's having a mind that is *fixed* on the love of God and the faith to believe He will supply everything we need. It's a peace that believes He is in total control and He will deal with our circumstances and with our enemies.

Psalm 112: 1—

Psalm 112:1 is the introduction to many blessings and promises from God **because** the hearer delights in God. We can't have peace if we're not delighting in God.

Psalm 112:6-8—

This peace is peace with God in Christ through His blood. It's not always felt, received, and enjoyed in the soul; yet the foundation of it always is, and is perfect. This peace is true, real and solid.

"No pilgrim is so well booted and buskined [well covered] as he who is at peace with God, his fellow men and his own conscience."[4]

Matthew 5:9—

Romans 12:18—

James 3:18—

Peace is a fruit of the spirit (Galatians 5:22). We have to sow it to reap it.

Psalm 34:14—

Isaiah 30:15—

Proverbs 14:30—

The gospel is light and life to those who believe in it and are willing to follow Christ in His death, His life, and His resurrection. We must be willing to die to *self*: our instincts and lusts, our moods and fleshly desires. If we have truly died to our *self*, we will grow in Christ and our fleshly desires will have "died" to the threatening things of this world that used to move us. We won't be so quick to react in our flesh but instead we will be securely grounded with our feet covered in the gospel of peace. The gospel is our solid foundation, just as the spiritual shoes or boots of the soldier were made of iron or brass. It keeps the soldier standing firm!

Zondervan NIV Study Bible, Isaiah 9:6, ©2002 The Zondervan Corp., Grand Rapids, MI

[2] John Gill, *Gill's Commentary*, Ephesians 6:15

[3] Charles H. Spurgeon, *Spurgeon's Devotional Bible*, Baker Book House Co. pg. 712

[4] Charles H. Spurgeon, *Spurgeon's Devotional Bible*, Baker Book House Co., pg. 712

Notes

SESSION SEVEN

"In addition to all this, take up the shield of faith, with which you can extinguish all the flaming arrows of the evil one."

Ephesians 6:16

As we continue to study the armor of God and look at Ephesians 6:16 we once again see that the Lord actually is our Spiritual Armor. He uses our faith in Him as a shield. It's still nothing we do. He is sovereign and He is ruling in our hearts.

When we are "walking by faith and not by sight" (2 Corinthians 5:7) He is our shield, protecting us from darkness and deception. We are believing the truth about our situations and resisting the lies because we believe Him to be who He says He is.

Psalm 3:1-3—

In Biblical days Roman soldiers used large shields covered with leather, which could be soaked in water and used to put out flame-tipped arrows. The analogy is: the enemy constantly shoots fiery arrows at God's people, but God is our shield. We will see that He truly is the One who will protect us.

Faith, like a shield, covers all and is therefore important above all. Look well to your confidence in God, for if this fails all fails.[1]

The shield may be understood as the grace of faith, which is like a golden shield, precious, solid and substantial; and like a shield of mighty men, by which many things are done, and by which the believer not only repels, but conquers the enemy.

We learn from the Scriptures that God is a shield:

Genesis 15:1—

The Jews say that repentance and good works are as a shield against divine vengenance;

faith in God is our shield; His power, His faithfulness, His truth that covers us is as a shield.

Psalm 5:12—

Proverbs 30:5—

Psalm 18:2—

God tells us exactly what we need to know to live out our lives for Him...He died for us, we should be living (lives of faith) for Him.

Luke 18:17—(Also found in Matt. 18:3, Mark 10:15)

Moreover, Christ is a shield and faith makes Him rise up as a shield, His person, His blood, righteousness, and sacrifice;[2] and all this opposes Satan's attempts. The Lord is the believer's protection and security. Christ's disciples have on the shield and fight the fight of faith and the shield is to be used in every conflict with any enemy.

Psalm 84:11—

Psalm 35:1-2—

Psalm 3:3—

Take this to heart: The devil *doesn't* have a shield, but we do! These verses we're studying speak for themselves! CHRIST IS OUR SHIELD! Lift Him up in your life!

"...with which you can extinguish all the flaming arrows of the evil one."

The evil one is, of course, Satan, who was the first wicked one and is the tempter of wickedness to others. He is wickedness himself and his temptations are the flaming arrows or fiery darts. They're called arrows or darts because they sometimes come suddenly and swiftly and thick and fast, and are very numerous, and where they stick are very troublesome and grieving.

These arrows/darts are fiery because they serve to inflame the mind, and to excite sin, as lust, anger, revenge, and the like; and were they not repelled, would be the occasion of bringing into everlasting burnings.

The shield of faith is of use to quench the fiery darts of Satans' temptations; so that they may not have the malignant influence they are designed for; which is chiefly done by faith's dealing with the blood of Christ. And there were ways of quenching the fiery darts – done by skins and hides of beasts made wet and anointed.[3]

We've just seen that a sacrifice had to be made to create a shield–something that would save us.

Think about it: in countless ways in Scripture we see the Lord speaking to us that salvation comes from Christ alone. It's His blood shed on the cross that provides our shield, our safety, our well-being, our life, our hope, our everything. His sacrificial death became our shield, quenching the scornful, fiery darts of our enemy. There is great power in the blood of Jesus Christ, and our enemy knows it!

We must daily *take up* that shield of faith and march on in obedience and love for Jesus Christ, our Commanding Officer.

Charles H. Spurgeon, *Spurgeon's Devotional Bible*, pg. 712, ©1998 Baker House, Grand Rapids, MI, .

[2] John Gill, *Gill's Commentary*, Ephesians 6:16, ©1980 Baker Book House, Grand Rapids, MI

[3] John Gill, *Gill's Commentary*, Ephesians 6:16, ©1980 Baker Book House, Grand Rapids, MI

Notes

SESSION EIGHT

"Take the helmet of salvation..."

Ephesians 6:17

This piece of armor is another analogy of the gospel: a helmet provides covering for our heads as Christ is the **Head** of the church, the **Ruler** of our hearts, the **King** of glory. The helmet protects us in our battles and covers our minds with the saving knowledge of Jesus Christ and His power. "Jesus" is "Yeshua" in Hebrew, which means "salvation". He is the author of salvation and the secured hope of it.

This hope of salvation by Christ is a defense of the head against false doctrines...and it raises and protects the head in times of difficulty, affliction and distress and it covers the head in the day of battle when engaged with Satan, the enemy of souls.[1]

God has given us protection (a spiritual helmet), so are we going to guard and rule over our thoughts? Our passage says "take" the helmet. We can't wait for someone to hand it to us or to put it on for us. We must take action and put it on! Look at what the Lord is saying to us:

1 Peter 1:13—

This a a graphic call for action.

Jeremiah 1:17—

Literally means "Tighten your belt around your waist!"

Job 38:3 (also Job 40:7)—

God is not humiliating or condemning Job but the implications are that Job is vindicated and eventually confirmed in ***Job 42: 7-9***.(NIV Study Bible Commentary). The point is, God was telling him to stand firm in his situation. Sound familiar?

Self-control is a fruit of the Spirit. God commands us to control our thoughts. The spiritual helmet will help us in this. "We can't tell how crooked our thinking is until we line it up with the straight edge of Scripture."[2]

The Scriptures tell us exactly how to control our thoughts and protect ourselves from the snares of the enemy:

Romans 12:2—

We should be desirous of daily reading, praying, praise and worship, and meditation, all of which are the opposite of conforming to this world. We have a tendency to forget that a person is not only committed to Jesus Christ for salvation, but is also committed, responsible, and accountable to Jesus Christ's view of God, the world, and of sin and the devil. This means that each person must recognize the responsibility to "be transformed by the renewing of her/his mind..."[3]

Ephesians 4:23—

2 Corinthians 4:16a—

"It is critical to distinguish between deceiving thoughts from the enemy and thoughts that are truly ours. If we think that tempting or accusing thought is our own, then we are going to reach some very bad conclusions about ourselves. God does not tempt us, but the devil will. Let no one say when he is tempted, 'I am being tempted by God'; for God cannot be tempted by evil, and He Himself does not tempt anyone" (Jas. 1:13). Jesus will never accuse you, because there is no condemnation for those who are in Christ Jesus (Rom 8:1.) But the devil "deceives the whole world (Rev. 12:9) and accuses believers day and night (v. 10)."[4]

2 Corinthians 10:5—

When we demolish strongholds, our thoughts clearly see Christ to be the lone, able, willing, full, and suitable Savior; we become obedient to Him, as both Savior and King. Such an enlightened soul looks to Him alone for life and salvation, joyfully and cheerfully receives and embraces all His truths and doctrines with faith and love, and obeys them from the heart...cheerfully and willingly submits to all His commands. He is carried captive, and not against his will, to be a voluntary subject of Jesus Christ, and cheerfully submits to the rule of His kingdom.[5]

We must see to it that we aid and assist God, and not stand against Him by saying, "I can't do that." God will not discipline us; we must discipline ourselves. God will not bring our "arguments ...and every thought into captivity to the obedience of Christ," we have to do it. Don't say, "Oh Lord, I suffer from wandering thoughts." ***Don't*** suffer from wandering thoughts. Stop listening to the tyranny of your individual natural life and win freedom into the spiritual life.[6]

We know what to do. God has spoken to us through His Word. He gives us what we need because we are His.

Philippians 4:8—

"Start loving the Lord with your mind. The Bible tells us to love the Lord with all our heart, soul, and mind. We need to make a living sacrifice of our mind as an act of worship. Meditate on God. Hold your mind to Him. I can't do it without help from God. I pray, 'Lord, make haste to help me.' He helps me and He will help you, too."[7]

The Bible says we must stand firm. It's an act of our will.

John Gill, *Gill's Commentary*, ©1980 Baker Book House, Grand Rapids, MI

[2] Elisabeth Elliot, www.goodreads.com/560173

[3] Oswald Chambers, *My Utmost for His Highest Updated Graduate Ed.*, ©1992 Discovery House Pub.,

[4] Neil T. Anderson & Dave Park, *Stomping Out Depression*, ©2001 pg. 128., Regal, Ventura, CA

[5] John Gill, *Gill's Commentary*, 2 Corinthians 10:5, ©1980 Baker Book House, Grand Rapids, MI[6] Oswald Chambers, *My Utmost for His Highest, Graduate Ed.*, Nov. 18

[7] Elisabeth Elliot, Gateway to Joy Radio Program, "Personal Discipline: The Discipline of the Mind," Oct. 30, 1989

Notes

SESSION NINE

"...and the sword of the Spirit, which is the Word of God;"

Ephesians 6:17

God has given us, by His grace, a very powerful weapon against the darkness: His Word. Imagine it as an razor-sharp, indestructible sword – a light saber – a weapon radiant and powerful enough to not only pierce the darkness, but to scatter it.

The Word of God is compared to a sword because it has two edges: the law and the gospel. The law convicts of sin, and cuts to the heart for it, and the other cuts down all the goodliness of man.[1] We are sinners in need of the Savior!

God's Word is called the "sword of the Spirit" because it is not carnal, but of a spiritual nature and is used by the spiritual man because it comes from the Holy Spirit. He provides us with and teaches us how to make use of it, and makes it powerful and effective.

Let's go to the source of all truth, the Bible, and we'll see a perfect example of the consistency of Scripture by looking at Ephesians 6:17 (our lesson) and Hebrews 4 :12.

Hebrew 4:12 – For the word of God is living and active. Sharper than any double-edged sword, it penetrates even to dividing soul and spirit, joints and marrow; it judges the thoughts and attitudes of the heart.

The author of Hebrews describes it as a *living power* that judges as with an all-seeing eye, penetrating a person's innermost being. The totality and depth of one's being.[2]

God's truth was revealed by Jesus (the incarnate Word; see John 1:1,14):[3]

John 1:1—

John 1:14a—

But in Hebrews 4:12, truth has been given verbally, too. This dynamic word of God is active in accomplishing God's purposes.[4]

Psalm 107:20—

Psalm 147:15—

[Personified as messengers commissioned to carry out a diving order.][5]

Psalm 147:16-18—

Look at this! The Lord of all creation secures His people's defenses and prosperity, their peace and abundant provision. These verses mention the whole range of weather.[6]

Isaiah 40:8—

The Lord Jesus Christ is always to be our example. Look how He handles this spiritual warfare when Satan came to tempt Him in the wilderness. Jesus' weapon of spiritual warfare was the sword of the Spirit: the Word of God.

Matthew 4:3—

Matthew 4:4—

Matthew 4:6—

Matthew 4:7—

[Satan tried to produce Scripture that would contradict itself and it never can. Also, he tempted Jesus to go outside the realm of His own safety and expect God, because He can keep him safe, to do it in spite of it being a foolish choice of behavior. The Hebrew word (wont) "tempt", is always taken in a negative way, because it tries the power, goodness, or will of God. NIV]

Matthew 4:8—

Matthew 4:9—

Matthew 4: 10—

Matthew 4:11—

When Jesus says, "It is written," He is not acknowledging the false and wrong citation of scripture made by the devil, nor of any misapplication of it; but mildly replies, by presenting another passage of Scripture to him. That's how we must respond.

The Bible is a bright, keen, pointed, well-tempered weapon, for offense and defense; it cuts a way for us through all foes, slays sin, and chases away even Satan himself. "It is written" is the terror of hell.[7]

God is equipping us "to stand" as He has been teaching us throughout this study. By His grace and His power we will continue to wave our radiant swords and keep on shining His Light. In His power we will be able to keep marching. He alone is trustworthy. He is our King and our Commanding Officer, and He is victorious!

---

[1] John Gill, *Gill's Commentary*, Ephesians 6:17

[2] *Zondervan NIV Study Bible*, © 2002 The Zondervan, Hebrews 4:12

[3] *Zondervan NIV Study Bible*, Hebrews 4:12

[4] *Zondervan NIV Study Bible*, Hebrews 4:12

[5] *Zondervan NIV Study Bible* Psalm 147:15

[6] *Zondervan NIV Study Bible* Psalm 147:16-18

[7] Charles H. Spurgeon, *Spurgeon's Devotional Bible*, C.H. Spurgeon, Baker Books, July 1988

Notes

SESSION TEN

"And pray in the Spirit on all occasions with all kinds of prayers and requests. With this in mind, be alert and always keep on praying for all the saints."

Ephesians 6:18

When we pray we glorify God. When we pray we look to the greatness of God and acknowledge that He is the One who has sovereign power over all things. When we pray we believe "...with man this is impossible, but with God all things are possible" (Matthew 19:26). And so we pray in faith. Something happens to us, too, when we pray. Think about it. Think about what happens to you when you pray often. Your focus is on Him and your relationship with Him.

Author/speaker Elisabeth Elliot believed, "God is God. Because He is God, He is worthy of my trust and obedience. I will find rest nowhere but in His holy will that is unspeakably beyond my largest notions of what He is up to." [1]

When we pray daily **with thanksgiving** in our hearts we are glorifying God, and our relationship with Him deepens and is enriched. We find our faith growing because we're spending more time with Him and we're seeing Him move through our prayers. The more we pray the more we "see" Him.

When we **are troubled** and we pray we are also glorifying God because we are saying, "Lord, I can't do it, I can't control it, I can't heal it, I can't fix it, but You can! So I call upon Your Name!" We are acknowledging the fact that God is the One. The Almighty. The All-Knowing. The All-Seeing. No one else can do what He can do.

"And pray in the Spirit on all occasions with all kinds of Prayers and requests."

He knows what we need. He invites us constantly to seek Him and to come to Him.

Philippians 4:6-7—

Anxiety and prayer are two great opposing forces in Christian experience. Thanksgiving is the antidote for worry, along with prayer and petition.[2] This is war, girlfriends; we must call out to Him when the fiery darts of fear and anxiety come at us! We've got to hold up that shield of faith and pray. He will answer!

Proverbs 15:29—

Prayer is part of our spiritual armor and is a powerful weapon. "*On all occasions with all kinds of prayers and requests*" includes mental and vocal, public and private prayers; petitions for good things, thanksgiving for mercies, the tearing down of evil strongholds in times of darkness, desertion, and temptations, and it should be used always.

In addition, our prayers should be prayed in the right spirit, with our heart, soul, and spirit engaged in it; with a true heart, without hypocrisy, in a spiritual way, with fervency and under the influence of the Spirit of God.[3]

He teaches us how to pray with the Lord's Prayer as our guide in Luke 11:2-5 and Matthew 6:9-13. He instructs us to begin with addressing the Father with praise and asking for His will to be done.

1 John 3:21-22—

1 John 5:14-15—

John 15:7—

Luke 11:9-10—

Psalm 27:14—

When we pray, we should pray in faith that God hears. This verse exhorts us to do that. God will accomplish His purposes. The peace that passes all understanding comes when we pray and then wait for God. Beware of what Oswald Chambers calls "spiritual lusting". Lust means "I must have it at once." Spiritual lusting causes us to demand an answer from God instead of seeking God Himself who gives the answer.[4] Whenever we insist God should answer our prayer in a certain way, we are off track. The purpose of prayer is to get ahold of God, not the answer.[5]

"With this in mind, be alert and always keep on praying for all the saints."

So, we're not to stop praying, according to Ephesians 6:18!

1 Thessalonians 5:16—

Luke 6:28—

Luke 18:1—

Read Luke 18:2-5—

Beware of thinking that intercession means bringing our own personal sympathies and concerns into the presence of God and then demanding that He do whatever we ask. Identification with God is the key to intercession, and whenever we stop being identified with Him it is because of our sympathy with others, not because of sin. It is sympathy with ourselves or others that makes us say, "I will not allow that thing to happen." And instantly we are out of that vital connection with God. **Vital intercession** leaves you with neither the time nor the inclination to pray for your own "bad and pitiful self". You do not have to struggle to keep thoughts of yourself out, because they are not even there to be kept out of your thinking. You are completely and entirely identified with God's interests and concerns in others' lives. God gives us discernment in the lives of others to call us to pray for them, never so we may find fault with them.[5]

Throughout Scripture, He invites us to pray. Are you picturing this? He is God and He is inviting us to draw closer to Him! He is at work through our prayers, 24/7, in everyday events and in the people around us. We have no idea the amazing things God is doing through our prayers — all the time, even now – for the prayers we prayed last week, or an hour ago, or last year. He is working through them.

When we are interceding for others—praying on their behalf, He is working. **We don't have to see it; we can be satisfied that we have spent time with God in prayer for someone and know He's going to answer that prayer in an amazing way**. He is always accomplishing His purposes. Believe it. He doesn't sleep! (Psalm 121:4) This makes prayer a very powerful weapon in our spiritual arsenal!

After spending this time together in God's Word, we can see that when we "put on" the full armor of God, we are "putting on" Christ!

We are called to be women.
The fact that I'm a woman does not make
me a different kind of Christian, but the fact that I am a
Christian makes me a different kind of woman. For I have accepted
God's idea of me, and my whole life is an offering back to Him of
all that I am and all that He wants me to be.
Elisabeth Elliot, Author
Let Me Be A Woman

---

[1] Elisabeth Elliot, *Through Gates of Splendor*, ©1996 Guild America Books

[2] John Gill, *Gill's Commentary,* Philippians 4:6-7

[3] John Gill, *Gill's Commentary,* Ephesians 6:18

[4] Oswald Chambers, *My Utmost for His Highest*, 2/7

[5] Oswald Chambers, *My Utmost for His Highest*, 5/3

Notes

AFTERWORD

A Faithful Christ Follower Lives a Supernatural Life

Women (and men, too, of course!) who follow Jesus live a supernatural life on earth because we each have the Holy Spirit of God living in us. It's the same Holy Spirit power that raised Jesus from the dead! This Holy Spirit in us consists of supernatural gifts. We can't see them or the power behind them with the natural eye, but we can with spiritual eyes! We see them and live them out with the eyes of our faith!

To glorify God and enjoy Him we must "walk by faith and not by sight" *(*2 Corinthians 5:7). When we're His we can see the effects of His presence and love in our lives and in the world. Oh, yes! But it is spiritual, supernatural.

> *The Apostle Paul wrote, "I pray the eyes of your heart may be opened ....so that you may know the hope to which He has called you...and His incomparably great power for us who believe. That power is the same as the mighty strength He exerted when He raised Christ from the dead..."*—**Ephesians 1:18-20**

> *By faith we believe He loves us unconditionally! Oh, how He loves us! "See what great love the Father has lavished on us, that we should be called the children of God! And that is what we are! The reason the world does not know us is that it did not know Him".* —**1 John 3:1**

> *By His Spirit, He teaches us truth and wisdom in His word when we read it. "Do not forget my teaching, but keep my commands in your heart, for they will prolong your life many years and bring you prosperity".*—**Proverbs 3:1-2**

> *By faith we trust He is always watching over us! "He will cover you with His feathers and under His wings you will find refuge; His faithfulness will be your shield..."*—**Psalm 91:4**

By constantly calling on His name and praising Him, He helps us in every way! He's given us the unexplainable gift of prayer as we journey through this life of painful valleys and exhilarating mountaintop experiences.

> *Our prayers operate through the power of the Holy Spirit in us. The Spirit tugs at our hearts to pray for someone or a family or even an entire city or country. So, we pray as we are led and faithfully persevere because we know our God is "able to do immeasurably more than all we ask or imagine, according to his*

power that is at work within us..."—**Ephesians 3:20**

There's that invisible power, again! Awesome, isn't it? Supernatural! We wait in faith for the answers to our prayers because we know God is always working behind the scenes. Look, when we're in Atlanta praying for people in China or Chicago, Alaska or Argentina, God will show up in those places through our prayers, in His time and for His purposes. Prayer to Almighty God is real and very powerful but we can't see Him as He changes the atmosphere. God tells us, "The prayer of the righteous is powerful and effective".—**James 5:16**

When God woos our hearts to become His child – He's the only one who really knows when we're ready to leave our old lives behind and call out to Him for the forgiveness of our sins. It happened to me. Everything changes for the better! Priorities. Choices. Habits. Lifestyles. We've changed. "Therefore, if anyone is in Christ, he is a new creation; the old has gone, the new has come! All this is from God who reconciled us to Himself through Christ...not counting people's sins against them".—**2 Corinthians 5:17-19**

Hallelujah! Now get ready for an ongoing spiritual battle. Jesus said, "If the world hates you, keep in mind that it hated me first" (John 15:18). We're not to be alarmed, we're to stand and shine! God has us covered with the full spiritual armor of God (Ephesians 6:10-18) for overcoming all things!

Everyone will hate you because
of me. But the one who stands firm
to the end will be saved.
Mark 13:13

ABOUT THE AUTHOR

Polly Balint is passionate about pointing other women to Christ so they could experience the supernatural, unconditional love of Jesus for themselves, as she abundantly enjoys. She's led Bible studies for women for many years: in churches, in the marketplace, and during conferences. She's hosted year-round women's studies in her own neighborhood for nine years. She's the author of a trilogy of devotional books, and recently published NURTURE, women encouraging women, we were made for this. She's a former freelance writer for national magazines, and a featured lifestyle writer for newspapers in South Florida and Georgia. She hosted a radio talk show at a local Christian station, interviewing difference-makers in the community. Polly and her husband, Don, live in Canton, Georgia, and have two beautiful adult daughters, one wonderful son-in-love, one hilarious grandson and one sweet rescue dog. For more information, visit **pollybalint.blogspot.com**, Instagram **@pollybalint**, or contact her as **authorpollybalint@gmail.com**.

Printed in the USA
CPSIA information can be obtained
at www.ICGtesting.com
LVHW081824300823
756768LV00011B/129

9 798890 411969